RIVERS

Nature's Wondrous Waterways

by David L. Harrison

Illustrated by Cheryl Nathan

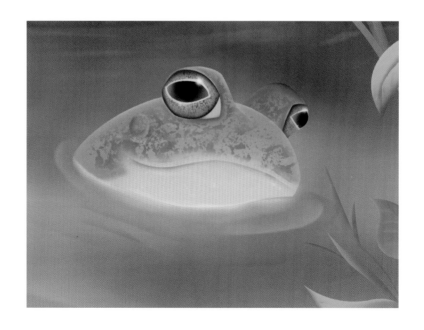

Boyds Mills Press

*The author wishes to thank Erwin J. Mantei, Ph.D., Professor of Geology,
Southwest Missouri State University, for his review of the original manuscript.*

Published by Boyds Mills Press, Inc.
A Highlights Company
815 Church Street
Honesdale, Pennsylvania 18431
Printed in China
Visit our website at: www.boydsmillspress.com

U.S. Cataloging-in-Publication Data
(Library of Congress Standards)

Harrison, David L.
Rivers: nature's wondrous waterways / by David L. Harrison ; illustrated by Cheryl Nathan.—1st ed.
[32] p. : col. ill. ; cm.
Summary: Explores the many elements that depend on rivers, both nature and people.
ISBN: 1-56397-968-3
1. Rivers — Juvenile literature. [1 Rivers.] I. Nathan, Cheryl, ill. II. Title.
551.48/ 3 21 2002 AC CIP
2001091105

First edition, 2002
The text of this book is set in 18-point Optima.

10 9 8 7 6 5 4 3 2 1

To Elaine Fry, our friend, who also loves nature
—D. L. H.

For my mother, Florence Nathan, with love
—Cheryl Nathan

Head across country
in any direction
and sooner or later
you'll come to a river.
That's what the pioneers did.
They needed water to survive,
and the best source of water
was a river.

A river meant water
for drinking, washing,
hunting, fishing,
farming, trapping,
and taking people
and their prized goods
to market.

So when they could,
settlers everywhere
built their towns
near rivers and lakes.

But people aren't
the only ones
who need rivers.
Armies of green
trees and plants
grow in rows
that line the banks
to be near water.

And too many tiny
creatures to count
are part of
nature's food chain.
Bugs eat plants.
Spiders eat bugs.
Frogs eat spiders.
Fish eat frogs.
Everyone gets
to eat something.

And when it rains
too much
and rivers flood,
bugs and plants
and bits and bites
from the food chain
in the water
help fertilize the fields
where crops will grow.

Some rivers flow
in wild places
where no one goes.
Some are deep enough
for ocean liners.
And some run on
for thousands of miles.

Where does all
the water come from?
How is a river made,
and where does it begin?
A river begins
in the mountains
where raindrops fall
on high hills
or drops drip
from ice and snow
or spill over banks
of lakes and ponds.

Some drops dry up
and return to the sky.
Some soak into the soil
and seep downhill
underground
through cracks
and holes in rocks.

Some run together
down the mountain.
From trickles
to rills
to streamlets
to streams,
those drops grow
into a river.

A young river
is full of energy.
It plunges and falls
this way and that
down the best path.
The charging water
scoops up dirt
and rolls and bounces
small rocks
as it splashes along.

Water pours in
from outer streams
and more arrives
from springs and caves
as the river flows
through low places
between hills.

The hills
and low places
make a valley
and all the water
in the same valley
drains down to
the same river.

As the river grows,
the force of its water
gouges a groove
called a channel.
It pries into cracks
and loosens pieces
of the mountain itself.
It may slice down
deep into rock
to carve a gorge
or a canyon.

It crumbles stone slabs
into pebbles and sand,
and cuts soft rocks,
creating riffles and rapids
and waterfalls.

The dirt and pebbles
and sand in the water
grind at the banks
and bottom
of the channel.
Scraping and bumping
and knocking along,
the river grows
wider and deeper.

As time passes,
and enough storms blast
and rains pound
and winters freeze,
parts of the valley
break off,
cave in,
or slide—
too slowly to see—
down to the water.

Over millions of years
the river and other
forces of nature
wear down the valley
and make its floor flatter.
Like a good trash hauler,
the river hauls off
the pieces.

Now the water
slows down
and wanders
back and forth
in lazy loops.
Here and there
it digs through banks
and cuts off loops
that leave
small lakes behind.

The water finds
the sea at last,
too sluggish to hold
its heavy load
of soil and sand
and debris.
The channel fills up
till it overflows.

So much water
makes marshy places
and many small rivers
that fan out toward the sea.
There it drops
the last of its load,
and billions of drops
from far-off mountains
finish their journey.

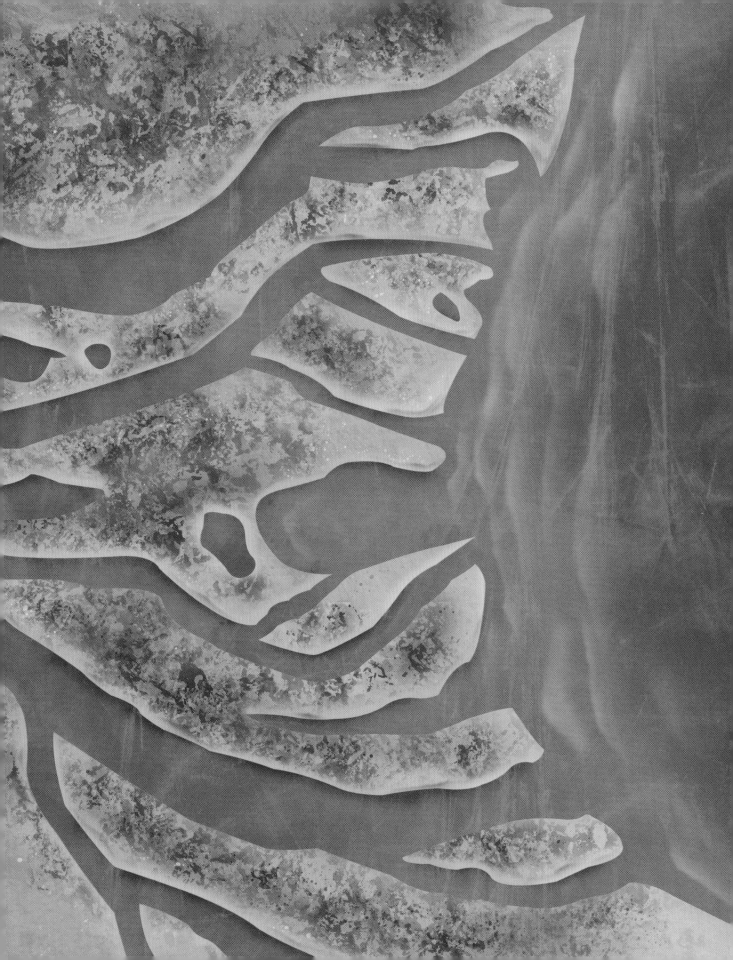

The mighty streams
we see today
have been around
a long time,
clearing the land
of debris
and extra water.
Nature depends
on rivers.

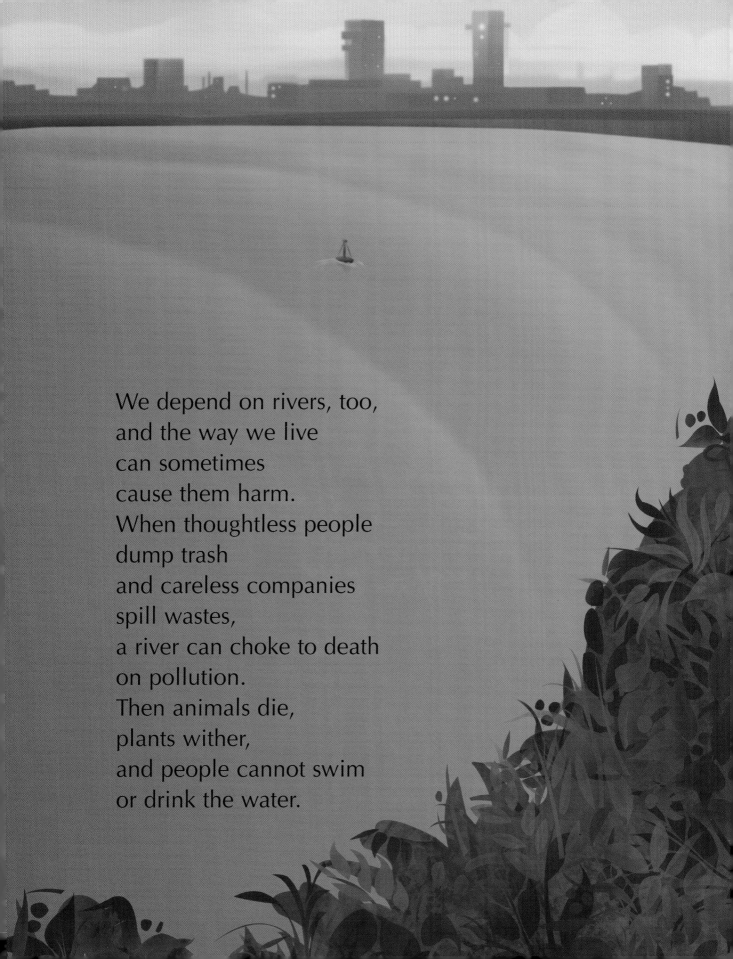

We depend on rivers, too,
and the way we live
can sometimes
cause them harm.
When thoughtless people
dump trash
and careless companies
spill wastes,
a river can choke to death
on pollution.
Then animals die,
plants wither,
and people cannot swim
or drink the water.

But even when
a river gets sick,
it can get well again.
When we clean up the water
and pick up the trash,
we can help a river
return to health.
Protecting our rivers
is everyone's job.
Nature depends on rivers.
We depend on rivers.
Rivers depend on us.

AUTHOR'S NOTE

From a place in the mountains, perhaps in a high meadow, a river is born. Hundreds or even thousands of miles later, it reaches the sea. The longest river in North America is the Mississippi-Missouri, which runs 3,892 miles and is the fourth longest river in the world. This book tells the story of what happens to a river along the way. But to get the best picture of why rivers are so important to the land and to life, it would help if we could stand back a little.

If we pretend we're riding in a satellite above the earth, we can see that groups of rivers form networks. Small streams join larger ones like branches of great trees, adding their loads of water and sediments to the growing rivers. All these streams and rivers play vital roles in nature. As mountains wear down and valleys form by erosion, rivers carry away the debris. When water evaporates from the sea and is carried in the atmosphere over the land where it falls as rain or snow, rivers return the excess water to the sea. These natural cycles have been going on for hundreds of millions of years.

We hope this book helps you want to learn more about rivers. Here are some other books you can read.

—David L. Harrison

FURTHER READING:

Carlisle, Norman. *Rivers*, Children's Press. 1982.

Dorros, Arthur. *Follow the Water from Brook to Ocean*, HarperCollins, 1992.

Hiscock, Bruce. *The Big Rivers: The Missouri, the Mississippi, and the Ohio*, Simon & Schuster Children's Publishing Division, 1997.

Knapp, Brian. *River*, Grolier Educational Corporation, (Series: Land Shapes), 1993.

Sauvain, Philip. *Rivers & Valleys*, Carolrhoda Books, Inc., 1996.

Tesar, Jenny. *America's Top 10 Rivers*, Blackbirch Press, Inc., 1998